WICKEN
A FEN VILLAGE

A Second Selection of Old Photographs

ANTHONY DAY

S.B. Publications

By the same author:
Turf Village (1983)
Wicken: A Fen Village in Old Photographs (1990)
Fen and Marshland Villlages (1992)
But For Such Men as These (1994)
Farming in the Fens (1995)

For Jean

First published in 1995 by S.B. Publications
c/o 19 Grove Road, Seaford, East Sussex BN25 1TP

ISBN 1 85770 099 6

Typeset, printed and bound by MFP Design and Print,
Longford Trading Estate, Thomas Street, Stretford,
Manchester M32 0JT.

CONTENTS

page

Front cover: Emma Aspland makes a charming composition of this family threesome before their farmhouse at Cross Green. They are Charles Cockrill, beer, wine and spirit agent, his wife Lydia and their daughter Eliza Anna. Lydia died on January 1st 1896 aged 76 and Charles died on March 13th 1905 aged 79. Eliza Anna lived later at The Poplars at the head of Chapel Lane where her relationship with farmer Robert Treen was intended to be more than polite. No matter how many times they met in a day, they would always shake hands, but that proved to be intimate enough for him. Eliza Anna died a spinster in 1936 aged 80.

Later Fred Marshall then Morley Hawes with his son-in-law Harold Crow farmed from this house, but all that remains of it now after alterations in the 1970s is the front wall and its windows and door. It is the home of Mr and Mrs Colin Searle.

(E.S. Aspland)

ACKNOWLEDGEMENTS

Apart from being indebted to so many Wicken people and those with close ties to the village, I am grateful for specific information received recently from Miss M.R. Barton, Henry and Mary Barnes, Brenda Place, Pearl Brown and Roland Avey and can never take for granted the willing help given by Michael Petty, Chris Jakes and the staff of the Cambridgeshire Collection and the support given by Steve Benz of S.B. Publications.

THE AUTHOR

Anthony Day is a professional landscape painter who also writes. He studied art at the Cambridge School of Art from 1948 to 1952 and at Reading University from 1954 to 1955, thereafter specialising in painting the fen country and its towns, selling his work through dealers in London and East Anglia and mixed exhibitions such as the Royal Academy and the Royal Society of British Artists.

For fourteen years he was art critic to the *'Cambridge Evening News'* but he is now principally interested in writing about country matters and local history. Recent articles by him have been published in *'The Countryman'* and *'Cambridgeshire Life.'* He has assembled a huge archive of photographs of his native village of Wicken which he used in books, exhibitions and slide-shows and took part in the important *'Fen Archive'* exhibition at the Cambridge Darkroom gallery in 1986, the catalogue of which is now a collectors' item.

INTRODUCTION

While the photographs in this second pictorial survey of life in Wicken span more than a hundred years I always hold hopes of finding others earlier, showing us our village as it was, either from the camera or the artist's hand. Aside from showing artefacts from prehistoric times, I have been able to go back before the age of photography only because four men of our village achieved fame enough to justify having their portraits painted. It was particularly rewarding to uncover these portraits and with them the ready information that goes with men of distinction.

Between their time and the arrival of the camera I have found little of worth; no evidence of any artist coming this way intent on recording the scene before the arrival in the 1870s of Robert Farren and his close friend Robert Macbeth A.R.A. who produced paintings and etchings of Wicken, Upware and the fens in general, preceding all but a few camera views by a mere decade.

It is no small miracle that the earliest photographs I show here survived at all. The portrait of Richard Peak, for instance, a wonderful discovery, was on glass and it stood relatively unguarded on a mantle shelf for ages before Gladys Smith, his granddaughter, carefully wrapped it away for posterity, the original going to the police museum. Most of us have lost cherished photographs of a much later date than 1852. With my conserving instinct I still wonder how I lost hold of some of the family snaps I knew. Some, of course, just wear away with use, some get marked by idle children, some vanish seemingly into thin air.

So often I wish I had begun the research much earlier, tapping an earlier generation for information and identifications. So often I have been greeted by my providers with: 'You should have begun this sooner. Dad would have told you all about that!' So would my grandad if I had got past his deafness, although his sight was too poor for photographs. I should be thankful for starting as soon as I did, some thirty years ago, expecting to exhaust the supply within a few years in a village of fewer than seven hundred inhabitants, a level maintained for over a hundred years, even through the recent trend for development. But pictures are still coming to light in surprising numbers so that this village's past must be covered pictorially as well as any in the land.

As in the first volume I cover the village roughly from east to west but include more portraits and groups. The school groups have an extra poignancy since we have now lost our school and another vital element of village life. At least I no longer have to exhort the teachers to continue having groups of children photographed, a custom that was discarded officially in the I960s. They served better than any census to record the population and ,of course, they grow more fascinating with time.

Wicken has survived well in its centre, but so much has been lost beyond it as these pictures must show. So many of those enchanting old farmhouses shown here need not have come down, but as this century unfolded they became fussy relics that people wanted to lose in the name of progress. Now we know that if by design or accident they had survived they would now be cherished. They would be worth a fortune too which is the way this century estimates worth. Emma Aspland's route to Padney in not now a pretty sight.

Ours is an age of over-tidiness and order with a contingent fear of letting nature take hold. Foreign shrubs displace the English growth and the sense of Englishness is on the wane. The age is slow to re-learn.

These pictures show the greater sensitivity of the past and I hope they encourage people to reflect upon it. The first volume was well received and I hope this second will satisfy as much.

EARLY HOMO SAPIENS

While farming from Field Farm on the Upware Road Frank Fuller was dedicated to retrieving ancient relics from the surface of the land. If always a joy to find old keys, coins and tokens dropped by our earlier generations and to see the signs of their old buildings, waterways and ponds rise to the top, it was even more rewarding to pick up the tools and weapons of primeval man and to carry them home to his extensive collection. Here we see a selection of axeheads, arrowheads and tools that inevitably withstood the rigours of time and climates so much better than more recent objects made by man. Thus we are left with a huge time gap between the earliest evidence of civilisation here and the latest of which we have adequate record.

(Peter Cook)

1

THE CHURCH OF ST. LAURENCE

Ours is one of four churches in Cambridgeshire dedicated to St. Laurence, who was one of the seven deacons of Rome. Driven to hand over the treasures of the church, Laurence had the courage to offer the sick and the poor as its treasures, for which he was roasted on a gridiron, which is his traditional symbol in church art. Although built on relatively solid foundations well above the fen level the church has needed constant restoration. Drastic reinforcement had to be undertaken in the 1960s to keep the north aisle upright, the last cause of its subsidence probably being the mighty explosion that demolished Soham station, less than a mile-and-a-half away, in June 1944. The church is of 13th century origin but much of it is of later date, the windows being Perpendicular in style. In the south aisle are brasses to the Peytons of Wicken and Isleham, Margaret obit 1414 and John obit 1520, and slabs in the chancel to the Cromwells, including Henry, of whom more later. This study of the church dates from 1934 and was used with a Cambridgeshire Planning Report stressing the need to retain all the trees. The first four along the front were however later removed.

(Author's collection)

EDWARD SIMPKIN'S HOUSE

Before this house at Cross Green was bought by Eddie Simpkin, pork butcher and grocer, it had three dwellings under the one roof. My great grandparents, William and Caroline Day, lived in the one on the right, George Nixon in the middle and Mary Day, William's spinster sister, at the other end. Eddie later added a plain brick shop to the right of this property, his slaughterhouse being in a shed at the other end, which was a deal better than slaughtering pigs on the green in front of gawping children. Eddie's father, John 'Thatcher' Simpkin, stands left and Eddie is holding the other hand of Alec, his lastborn, who was to succeed him in the business after gaining experience in Cambridge. Alec's mother died six weeks after he was born and it is Eddie's daughter, Nartha Jane (later Firman of Hucknall), standing behind, who is acting as housekeeper and nanny. On the right is another Simpkin, Bill, the village carpenter and undertaker, clearly doing repairs in the year 1901. Eddie Simpkin married again. The dwelling has now been elaborately restored, minus the original thatch that was not allowed.

(E.S. Aspland)

3

THE GALE

A gale struck the village in 1906, removing the gable end of the cottage on the right, which brought the photographer to the village for this grainy photograph, the only print of it I have found. The picture also reveals the state of the road at that time. Two years on Mr Cole Ambrose of Fordy Farm on the outskirts of the village had a row of horsechestnut and sweet chestnut trees planted alongside the street by the Maid's Head green where most of them remain. They became vital to us boys hoarding dead leaves for Guy Fawkes' night. The tall tree in the centre is also a horsechestnut, giving its name to the cottage behind. An insurance dispute led to its being felled after the last war. The house on the left was replaced in the 1960s by a larger facsimile.

(Author's collection)

THE CORONATION

There is a fair turnout here passing Cooper's Row in the high street for the coronation of George V on June 22nd 1911 with a makeshift band leading outside the picture. Wicken Wesleyan Brass Band, founded in 1869 ,had long since disbanded and with no other band available for this day a call went out for empirical instrumentalists to come forward. Along came one cornet (Walter Bishop), one euphonium, two piccolos (one Bill Barnes), one tin whistle, one flageolet (Bill Simpkin), one bass drum, one kettle-drum and one violin, plus one harmonium (Jemima Simpkin) to be carried in a turf cart drawn by sturdy lads. The march behind them to church and back was followed by sports and a few musical items in a field in Butts (Drury) Lane. The players so enjoyed it that they came together again to form a true brass band, back by a loan of money from the vicar, the Reverend Ernest Dibben. They progressed to become Wicken Coronation Silver Prize Band and they are thriving today. This photograph was taken from the bedroom window of Charlie Cranwell's cottage on the corner of Butts Lane showing at the right in the foreground Mrs Martin Bailey, trying to hide a blemish on her chin, and beside her Mr and Mrs John Sargeant with Mrs Barber pushing the pram in front. The nearest boys in the column are Billy Avey, George Cranwell and Alec Simpkin.

(Author's collection)

5

THE BAND IN 1921

Behind the Back Way (now Back Lane), not far from the mill, lay the broad pasture, 'The Weights,' owned by the miller, Woollard Barton. It was the scene for the Fellowship Sports every summer until the village fetes split the interest in the one occasion. The walnut trees aligned across the pasture are here giving shade to the band on the sports day of July 1921, the year that also saw the production of 'A Midsummer Night's Dream' by a troupe from Burwell between the great elms that stood in the low part of the pasture. While understanding little of the play many of the audience admired the acting and costumes. It may well have been that those elms were saplings when the play was written. They succumbed to Dutch Elm Disease in the 1970s. The formation of the band in 1921, that summer of drought, was as follows, left to right, back row - Luke Rumberlow, Henry Clay, who was minus a leg and could never march, Giley Bailey, George Avey, Reg Bailey, Bert Canham, George Barton, Albert Avey, Alec Simpkin and Harry 'Rocker' Norman. Seated - Charlie Avey, Arthur Scrivener, Billy Avey, Nathan Norman, Joe Clay and Albert Taylor. Kneeling - Arthur Andrews, Ernie Avey and Horace Clay.

(Author's collection)

DAVID BARTON

Living next door to John 'Bunyan' and Sarah Bailey at the west end of Cooper's Row between 1890 and 1912 was David Barton, third son of Shaw and Mary Barton, who was one of three young men wanting to better themselves in the New World. A close pal of Bert Bailey, his neighbour, he was soon telling him of his plans to emigrate to America with Arthur Taylor and Sidney Day, my uncle. Their embarkation date was fixed and they bid farewell to family and friends. But, to his acute embarrassment, David was soon home again, sent there after a medical inspection to recover from a possibly contagious blemish on his face. He tried again, but too soon and was forced to wait longer. Then, while his pals wondered on the other side, he was accepted aboard the 'Titanic' and perished at sea on April 15th 1912. Arthur Taylor returned home for a visit but Sidney Day never returned. Both worked for the Kodak Company in Rochester and their families survive them.

(Author's collection)

HIGH STREET, 1912

Four years after their planting the Cole Ambrose trees are well established and the road is in sounder condition. The scene is very little different today, although after road widening the footpath is on the inside of the trees. Beyond them on the corner of Butts Lane is the shop kept by Charlie Cranwell senior, whose father Robert was the first occupant of the cottage who used the shop building as a cobbler. It was only very recently removed in the cause of very sympathetic modernisation. In the distance there were no buildings from Cross Green to the church, a stretch, earlier lined with trees, known as 'The Carsa' (causeway).

(Author's collection)

HIGH STREET, 1920s

The peace of the village is captured in this view from the mid-1920s, maintained by the absence of traffic as we know it today. The chestnut trees are well advanced here some seventeen years after planting. A leisurely chat in the middle of the road such as this is impossible now and, of course, the road is out of commission as the playground that served us so well in my childhood. There we burned off energy playing hopscotch, skipping, bowling hoops that were seldom other than old tyres or wheels and lashing spinning tops as best we could from one end of the village to the other. The school playground was too constricting for such exercises. The cross placed on the far gable end on the left was put there by Rosa Stevens to indicate to her sister Bella, living in South Africa, the new retirement home bought by their parents, Arthur and Louisa Stevens, formerly of the Swaffham Engine, Upware. When Bella came home for a visit in 1933 she brought a name plate for the cottage, 'Tembani' after an African village made by her husband, a gilder. It was discarded a few years ago. Cooper's Row on the left had lost its unity to individual tastes but the cottages at each end have, happily, been cleaned down to the brickwork.

(Author's collection)

HOSPITAL SUNDAY, 1922

The turnout for the parade to church and back on Hospital Sunday, coinciding with Wicken Feast on May 13th, involved a huge proportion of the population, plus many others arriving on bikes. The village policeman and local dignitaries led the parade followed by the band, ex-servicemen, the fire brigade from Soham and Fordham, decorated wagons or lorries and those huge banners proclaiming the benevolent societies. Special teas preceded the intermingling during and long after the parade and the pubs did a good trade afterwards to the disapproval of the majority. Here in front of Harry Page's bakery, yards in front of our house at Cross Green, the column has broken up. In the foreground Mary Bailey holds her sister Nora in her right hand and Nelly Bailey in her left. Beyond the man with his back to them are Bert and Walter Canham. The clear face at the rear of the horse is Fred Hall. The tiny girl, white against black, at the right is Pearl Avey holding the hand of her mother, Lilian, with her father, Charlie, behind.

(Shepherd, Soham)

HOSPITAL SUNDAY, 1932

Fashion has moved on, for the farm wagon has given way to the lorry for the decorated float seen before Tembani Cottage aforementioned. The owner of the lorry, Jesse Lofts of Fordham, a builder, stands left with his wife in the cabin. Mr Lofts built the bungalow in North Street owned by Jack and Jessie Russell. It was built for the late Reg 'Wick' Alsop, a native of Wicken whose benevolence served the village so well, and intended for his mother but he sold it on. On the wagon, shily presenting themselves, left to right are Muriel Bailey as Britannia, then Eileen Blackmore, Dorothy 'Jim' Barnes, Joan Gandy, Winnie Barnes (back), Jessie Clay, Albert Shaw, Gladys Bullman, Don Bullman, Roland Avey with Mrs Ben Shaw, left, and Mrs Clements in front. The one bandsman in view, with trombone, is Bert Canham, enlisted since the previous picture.

(Pearl Brown collection)

BUTTS LANE COTTAGES 1903

On the site of the present bungalow owned by Mr and Mrs Don Delph stood these cottages with the outbuildings of the Maid's Head behind. After their demolition the area was used as a farmyard by Solomon Hurst who lived opposite. The lady left is Rose Bailey who later married Albert King. She is holding Fred, the child of her sister Nell, whom she brought up. She had no children of her own. From the left is Eliza Bailey, who lived here and later lived in the Afterway cottages, with her daughter lsabella lrene, Mrs Coe and Nell Bailey herself. The second child from the left is Alice Hall, later Burden living in London. A renowned miser known as Bob Trots was found dead in one of these cottages where his hoards of gold, silver and copper were concealed in various crannies . Levi Bullman senior lived in the far cottage.

(E.S.Aspland)

12

THE GREENS

Wicken is lucky in its spread of grass in the centre of the village, originally common grazing land separated into Cross Green, where the remains of the stone cross mark the site of the market place, the Maid's Head Green, the Mission Hall Green, as we now know it, and Pond Green. And this indeed is how they were cropped right up to the second world war. Where there was such plentiful grass the cattle, horses or donkeys would never stray far but in course of time, with the occasional motor vehicle passing through, a boy would be offered reward for minding them for the farmer. When playing on those greens between the wars we had to be careful where we were treading, but my infancy was accompanied by the comforting sound of cows munching right up to and even off our hedge and the strong odour they left behind. Donkeys were best where thistles grew, as they once did on the Mission Hall Green. Bill Norman's shop stands behind in this view of the Maid's Head Green in the 1920s, this being one of the picture postcards he sold. He was also a coal merchant and had some land and turf pits. Much of my back garden was once his and it still yields lumps of coal, nails and links, not to mention glass from the hoard of bottles dating back beyond his tenure, those intact dug out by Stanley Fenton during his time as an antique dealer in the shop.

(Author's collection)

13

THE CORN MILL

The great job of restoring Wicken's mill into full working order is gradually nearing completion. The group of devotees are now building new sails from scratch and among the enthusiasts is Jacquie Ward, a descendant of the first miller there in 1813, arriving with her husband at every opportunity to lend a hand. In this view of the mill early this century we are in the time of Woollard Barton, standing right with the scoop. Beside him is Bob 'Fal-lal' Simpkin, former postman and fetcher of medicines from Soham across the mere and the last village crier, who lived adjacent where Trudy Bristow lives now. Engine power had already arrived to drive the mill on windless days, as we see here. A shed with an oil-powered engine was later installed. The mill closed down soon after the outbreak of the second world war but its purchaser, George Johnson, continued to use it as a store before selling it to the restorers rather than those who wanted to convert it to a quaint home.

(E.S.Aspland)

VIEW FROM THE MILL

Not much of the village can be seen from the top of the church and the only other high vantage point excepting trees was from the top of the mill. Leslie Boning, a frequent visitor to the 'Five Miles' inn at Upware, pointed his camera from it in 1915, recording so much that has since disappeared, including all the foreground buildings. At that time Nathan Norman and his family lived in the one on the right and Jaby Bell's cottage shows beyond. Jaby was an ace pig-slaughterer who did the job, using only a knife, on Cross Green. The thatched house was the home of Fred 'Stubby' Bailey, turf-digger and the one beyond housed Charlie Avey and family at the near end and & Susan Clay at the other. It is King's Lane beyond it and the outbuildings down which lived Billy and Liz 'Puddn' Bailey and, facing the Back Way, Jake Barton. Soham Mere in the distance, now a bare open space, had many trees across it at this time.

(Leslie Boning)

THE BASKETMAKER

Charlie Avey was born in Ashley near Newmarket, the son of Edward, a butcher. He spent his early working days as a brewer's drayman in London but he married Lillian Clay of Wicken, seven years his junior, on June 8th 1896 and they had nine children. Seven were sons who at one point formed the nucleus of Wicken Band, of which Charlie was a founder member. An injury by a farm roller in his youth left him disabled in one leg. At one time he worked in the fruit orchards between Wicken and Burwell, forming an alliance with Ally Gilbert whose own handicap was a short arm. These two found a rhythm of work to suit their disabilities moulding up the asparagus beds between the trees, earning piecework wages above the average. Charlie then succumbed to tetanus, an accepted fatal disease then, but he astonished Addenbrooke's hospital and the village by recovering. His eldest son Billy attended basket-making classes at Mr Walling's night school and roused his father's interest in the craft, who then sought further training from Benjamin Bradshaw, the basketmaker living in Pratt Street, Soham. Charlie soon became adept at the craft using a shed fronting his cottage on the corner of King's Lane. Later, after moving to the council houses, he used a shed behind the vicarage where he had a one-acre allotment. Apart from the selection of his wares we see here, in his early days he wove instrument cases for his beloved band and a basketchair to be towed like a rickshaw behind the cycle of shoemaker Morley Houghton, to allow his ailing wife to take the air. Charlie died in 1952 aged 82, two years after his wife.

(Pearl Brown collection)

THE POND

The main alteration to this scene since the time of this photograph in the 1920s has been the planting of trees by the pond. . Four saplings appear here, placed in line with the hedge, but I cannot recall their survival. Fern Cottage stands right, having in 1913 replaced a thatched dwelling, with Providence Cottage next to it and Chestnut Cottage next. On the left is Honeysuckle Cottage and the next is mine, The Mangle House, so named after the occupant, Jemima Bailey, acquired a big iron mangle to take in washing. She left the mangle - and the house on condition he paid £40 for it - to the village blacksmith, William Rose, but the mangle remained in the cottage for further use into recent living memory. They are domestic ducks on the pond, owned by James Day living in the house now owned by Bob Porter. This view was sold as a picture postcard by Bill Norman

(Author's collection)

THE FARMYARD

Soon after his wife's death in 1930, James Day, my grandfather's brother living in this farmhouse facing the pond, sold the property to Harry Vincent Towell, who had come in from Birmingham to take over the shop in North Street formerly owned by Arthur Bullman and Francis Easthaugh. Earlier James Dennis then James Bullman farmed from here. This picture was taken by Mr Towell's daughter Kathleen, who later returned to Wicken to become its schoolmistress, then parish clerk living in Burwell. It shows her sister Margaret enjoying her calm role on a fine summer's day, but it also shows the good condition of the house, the waterbarrow by the fence, the mare with its sprig to ward off the flies by movement and the dog 'Scamp' enjoying the freedom of most dogs then. Bob Porter worked for Mr Towell here and he later bought the premises.

(Kathleen Towell)

18

THE PUMP

It still stands at the top of Pond Green, a non-functioning relic, one of our sources of drinking water before piped supplies came in 1946. Here, circa 1920, Bert Burgess of Luton poses by the pump for Major Hare, the son-in-law of the then Wicken vicar, the Reverend Lewis. Burgess had been organist to the Reverend Lewis when he was at Luton and he visited him often at Wicken and while here he played the organ in our church. In the background the Red Lion is still under thatch as is James Day's large barn behind his farmhouse. The lamp-post by the pond had not carried its oil lamp since the first world war when they were extinguished for good.

(Major Hare)

19

RICHARD PEAK

Local constables, paid by the parishioners, were the arms of the law in our villages before county police forces were formed. Wicken received its first uniformed policeman from the outside in 1851, a native of Dunmow in Essex, P.C. Carlow. A single man, he resided here with Mr and Mrs John Goodall, a respected couple and managed well enough within the wall of suspicion that inevitably, surrounded him. Insularity was strong here, with but one sound road into and out of the village until 1928. Carlow stayed for a year-and-a-half, moved to Isleham then gradually climbed the ranks to become a Superintendent in the south Cambridgeshire village of Arrington, where he retired and settled. His successor in Wicken had a worse reception. P.C. Richard Peak, born in Caxton in 1832, for his youth mainly, incurred resentment from the start. The bareness of his charge book to the end implies intimidation. Here he is in 1852, proud enough of his new uniform to have himself photographed in it while the technique was still in its infancy. On Friday August 17th 1855 he was present at a hay sale at the Red Lion inn, staying until 3.15 a.m. at the behest of the landlord in order to restrain the last noisy drinkers. Richard lived in Burwell with his young wife and son, safely outside the centre of his duty, but he never finished the two-mile walk home that morning and the mystery of his disappearance remains.

(Cambridgeshire Police Museum)

ANN DENNIS PEAK

From his previous centre of duty in Kirtling near Newmarket Richard Peak courted Ann Dennis Cooper of Soham, daughter of a shopkeeper, where they married in the Independent chapel on March 3rd 1854. Settled in Burwell with their son she was soon set wondering at her husband's long absence on the morning of August I7th and set off the alarm. Richard had not foreseen his long night's work, for he had anticipated a fair night's sleep before meeting up with the neighbouring patrol at 4.a.m. at the north end of Burwell. His non-arrival caused no concern since individual duties always came first, but soon an exhaustive search for him was begun. It yielded nothing. Rivers and ponds were dragged, the countryside scoured, the ports of the kingdom were informed and wild rumour took over. The claim that his body was cast into the brick kiln near Wicken Sedge Fen was refuted by the police who had recognised the innocence of the two men on duty at the kiln that night and tales of brass buttons being raked from the ash were dismissed because Richard was not wearing any that night. To save their uniforms policemen were encouraged to wear private clothes as often as possible and this did not diminished their authority. When he walked from the inn Richard was wearing a brown straw hat, a brown greatcoat a check coat, a dark cloth vest, a pair of coarse uniform trousers, black necktie and Wellington boots - quite a covering for the season. He also carried his official staff and a pair of handcuffs. That he was set upon and murdered seems certain, although murder may not have been intended. Ann Dennis Peak with her son Sidney moved back to Soham with her parents where she maintained herself as a dressmaker.

(Gillian Peak collection)

THE MURDERED MAN'S CHILDREN

Ann Dennis Peak was carrying their second child when her husband
disappeared and she was left to bring up the two boys within the home of her
parents, Mr and Mrs Joseph Wood Cooper, who kept a general stored at Cross
Green, Soham. The elder boy, Sidney William, standing right, became a painter
and decorator, undertaking general household repairs and well-sinking in
Soham, where he died in 1933. The second son, Alfred, became a printer
working in London, but he died young. Ann Dennis Peak died in 1904, a
woman haunted by the mystery of her husband's fate. Sidney Peak's daughter
Gladys became a schoolteacher whose own husband, after they had been
married but two years, met a tragic end. She, Gladys Smith, preserved these
family mementoes

MARK BAILEY'S COTTAGE

There is nothing to match the charm of the thatched cottage kept in good repair and this one looks set to last for ever in the 1870s. Yet in my childhood such came to be held in contempt as symbols of decay and poverty and little compunction was felt in taking them down, often to be replaced with brick and slate or tile dwellings. Such happened here to Sycamore Cottage, replaced by the present house at the top of Pond Green in 1903. Here stands Mr and Mrs Robert Lister, whose daughter Ellen (1844-1921) married Mark Bailey (1845-1913) of Wicken, farmer and turf merchant, in 1867, settling here, although there were two dwellings under this one roof. The charming cottage behind was also removed but not replaced. What would they have been worth today!

(Author's collection)

THE SYCAMORES

Here we have probably the oldest dwelling in Wicken, disregarding the origins of the Hall and Spinney Abbey, Hopefully The Sycamores, of Tudor origin, facing the Mission Hall green, will truly last for ever, for it is a seat of local history and held fond memories for James Wentworth Day, the author of country books, who lived in it throughout his childhood. He reflects on it thus in the preface to his 'History of the Fens' in 1954: 'When one lay in bed, under that roof of deep thatch, the moon striking white through a poke-bonneted window in whose rounded eaves sparrows slept, snug as mice, there came through that window, in the witch hours before dawn, the smell of the fen. A strange, indefinable smell, scent of reeds and peaty waters, of sallows and meadowsweet, of rotten filly pads - and of fish.' Alas, the smells are not that pure today with the artificial means of preserving the fen wet, the damming in of dead water, the fear of disorder for the visitors. But nothing purer these days would penetrate the traffic fumes afflicting The Sycamores.

(Gillson, Burwell)

HOME FROM SCHOOL

High Street extends to Chapel Lane and just past that point these children are on their way home from school in 1932. They are Terry and Gloria Harding pushing the wheelchair and Chrystal Harding in front. Doug Clements in the chair had arrived with his family from Fordham to live in a council house. An early illness took away the use of his legs and further spells in hospital did nothing to improve them and merely interrupted his education. He was immensely likeable and popular and happy to let us boys treat his wheelchair as a motor car. He became a skilled technician without any support to develop it. The council would not allow him to have a workshop in the garden and there were no means to train him further. He merely furthered his craftwork on the floor of the kitchen with his mother's huge support. After her death he moved to Soham pursuing an interest in photography but he died aged 44. In the background of this view we see Peartree Cottage, the Jubilee Almshouses and the Mission Hall. The rebuilt almshouses are modelled on the old and the scene is little changed today.

(Author's collection)

THE ENTERTAINERS

Originally built and consecrated as a second church conveniently placed in the centre of the village, the Mission Hall of 1887, built by subscription to coincide with the Queen's Golden Jubilee, soon became the all-purpose village hall, increasingly put to the service of self-entertainment. Between the wars in particular there was much enterprise in this field and this concert group of 1921 put a lot into their rehearsals and costumes. They are, at the back left to right: Alec Simpkin, Vera Marshall, Wilfred 'Boy' Barton, Monica Ruby Barton, Dorothy Jenkinson, Tom Fuller and Albert Avey. Seated. Gladys Norman, Dorothy Marshall, Arlene Easton who instructed them in dancing, Kate Taylor and Joyce Bailey. In front: Eunice Fuller and Rose Norman.

(Starr and Rignall)

THE TITBITS CONCERT PARTY

Wicken's silver, jazz and mouthorgan bands all strove to warm up the winter evenings in the hall between the wars but, in an age of concert parties, there was no local group more dedicatedly up with fashion than the Wicken Tilbits Concert Party, who also travelled to entertain. Here they are at the Houghton Hall in Cambridge in the early 1930s after giving a concert there. The hall caretaker standing right is Fred Johnson, son of the Wicken cobbler Peachey Johnson. Fred lived in Cambridge as did Stan Granfield, standing right, who was then a teacher at St. Luke' school and who later became headmaster of Romsey Primary School and a Cambridge councillor. Stan continued to travel to Wicken ~on a motor cycle twice a week in the interests of this group. Titbits took over from The Co-optimists in Wicken and from left to right, seated, they are: Albert Avey, Dorothy Jenkinson, Eunice Fuller, Joyce Bailey, Vera Marshall, Blanche Bailey, Joe Norman and Gwen Granfield. Missing is George Cranwell, the comic turn, who sometimes teased the others by dressing inappropriately for the parts. Having done so on this night he was chided so severely he took umbrage and refused to face the camera.

(Author's collection)

EMMA SOPHIA ASPLAND

Living at The Chestnuts opposite Chapel Lane, where her forebears had been as shopkeepers since the I740s, Emma Sophia Aspland (I87I-I948) was the last of her family line there. She remained unmarried but appears a very presentable young lady here in the I890s, a study I have taken from a group which is the only true portrait I have found of her. This is sad since she served the village and its character so well with her dedication to the camera. Some seventy confirmable studies of hers have turned up but never a negative and never the camera or cameras. So much of Wicken would have been lost to view but for her. She could have made photography her profession but had no need to work and she seemed to do her best to conceal her gift. She remained a remote, withdrawn figure in my childhood, keeping close company only with the schoolmaster and his wife but sometimes giving her servant a rough time.

(Author's collection)

THE GREAT UNITARIAN

The most distinguished member of Wicken's Aspland family was the Reverend Robert Aspland (1782-1845), a renowned Unitarian pastor. His father Robert, the second generation in Wicken, had turned to the Unitarian faith and he converted an outbuilding at The Chestnuts into a place of worship. He invited the early Wicken Wesleyans to share this chapel until their own was built in the 1820s. His son Robert came under the devout influence of the village blacksmith living next door at the forge, John Emons, then left the village to study for his intended role in life as a minister of religion. Returning at the age of sixteen he preached in front of The Chestnuts to more than three hundred people. Eventually he became pastor at the Gravel Pit in Hackney, London, and remained there for more than forty years. His fame entitled him to be painted for our benefit. His son, Robert Brook Aspland M.A. followed him in his calling and wrote a biography of his father and his own son, Lindsay Aspland became a Queen's Counsel.

THE BLACKSMITH'S COTTAGE

John Emons lived in this cottage that has been the home of Wicken's blacksmiths for generations, and there is one there today in James Garton. He succeeded Walter Redit who was born in Wicken, but prior to him the last local-born blacksmith was Henry Treen. He gave way to William Rose, he to his son Ernie and then came Harry Bean, albeit living in Cooper's Row, and Arthur 'Bill' Redit who was born in Suffolk and served his apprenticeship in Burwell. In this view of June 1892 we see Mrs William Rose and Ernie gazing towards their skip beehives, a scene as poetic as a Samuel Palmer etching. In spite of the rigours of farm work there was no harder working member of the community than the blacksmith. He was the farrier too, of course, and wet days when the farmers could not get on the land could become a purgatory to him as horses were lined up to be shod and he could in no way turn away the work. Bill Redit worked on late into the evenings, allowing his forge to be a meeting place for resting landworkers. It was not a restful atmosphere with metal sparks flying off the anvil but the men barely deigned to flinch, although we boys had to watch our bare knees and heads.

(Birmingham Library Services; P.J. Deakin)

THE PATCHES

Taking the shortest route on foot, whether to school,work, church, chapel,the village pumps or neighbouring villages was instinctive in all villagers to save time, legs and the labour of carrying and that is why we had scarred greens and rights of way across, sooner than round, fields and through private properties. Some of Wicken's rights of way have been obscured and some are still under threat by individuals and groups, but a lot has been done recently to open them up. They are more useful to Wicken than to some other villages since the circuitous routes to Soham and Burwell increase the distance fourfold. Our footpaths and byways to Soham have been restored and it is surprising that so few use them. Once it was charm all the way across there, through The Patches at North-holt corner beyond Drury Lane and out through kissing gates on to the mere. The first intrusion into the charm of The Patches was a pillbox during the last war and there it remains. Its trees, hedges, pond and profusion of wild flowers fell to the plough in the I960s. Here in the early I930s, fetching his mares for work, aided by his son Sam, is Dick Bailey of Butts Farm.

(Author's collection)

WICKEN AMATEURS F.C.

While having previously brought together teams to play the occasional friendly football match, it was not until 1936 that a football club was formed in Wicken. It competed in the Ely and District Junior League and the first team was: Jacko Bullman, Bert Houghton, Ron Clay, George Scrivener, Denis Porter, Tom Norman, Wilf Day, Clifford Nixon, Joe Redit, Frank Aves and Billy Gilbert. After closure during the war they re-formed in 1946 but had to wait until I956 before winning their first trophy, the Wilkin Shield. This, left to right, is the team with the shield. *Back*: John Bailey, captain, Mick Harding, Roy Dennis, Bert Wesley, Charlie Harding, Cyril Dennis, Alan Nixon. *Middle*: John Taylor with club supporters Arthur Scrivener, Arthur Cornell and Alec Simpkin and Jim Nightingale. *Front*: Brian Diver, Godfrey Bird and Ray Harding. Playing at Moulton near Newmarket they had beaten Hilgay, Norfolk, in the final. The club, competing at a higher level now, first played on Slade Close in Church Lane (Road) and now in Chapel Lane where the field has recently been acquired by the parish council for the purpose of recreation.

(Author's collection)

SID LUCKY

Before having his house and shop built in 1913 in North Street, Sidney Canham, who was trained in shopkeeping by his true father, Arthur Bullman, across the street, mended cycles in a shed on this site. His further enterprises were many but he was concerned to delegate more and more of the work. After the second world war Sid decided to renovate his shop and here it is all white and shiny with no alterations to the original structure. After his time the shop changed hands several times and this shopfront was reduced to something much meaner, the remains of it still being there some five years after the shop's closure. At the time of this photograph there were four more such shops in the village, none of them now remaining.

(B. and S. Turner collection)

THE FIRE

This is what happened to Arthur 'Thumper' Bullman's general stores on March 6th 1913, the cause suspicious but never certain. The fire extended to the neighbouring cottage owned by Arthur and tenanted by James and Susan Canham, burning it to the ground. While his shop was being rebuilt Arthur continued business in the vacant shop attached to Butts Farm but not long after returning to his North Street premises he sold the shop to Francis Eastaugh and he to Harry Vincent Towell and he to Freddie Jenkins. The Cooperative Society ran the shop for a long time, after which its has changed hands several times and was last owned by Garry and Judith Petersen.

(Author's collection)

THE FIREFIGHTERS

These are the firefighters called out to Arthur Bullman's fire in 1913, gathered by their best source of supply, the village pond, pumping, by hand, of course, through one long pipe all the way down the street. The appliance was kept in Wicken, often in Olley Bullman's yard behind the cottage on the right, and was drawn by horses. There was no racing to fires from afar then and bicycles were the steeds here. On the extreme left is John Lockwood of Soham who drove the threshing engine for Fyson's. Beside him stands Ally Gilbert with his father Bob, who had moved as the camera clicked, and John Fuller. The two boys in front are, left, Stan Granfield when at Soham Grammar School and Tom Day, younger brother of James Wentworth. Just behind him is Bill Granfield. The building used temporarily by Arthur Bullman for his shop shows behind the Gilberts.

(Author's collection)

ALBERT HOUGHTON

You can tell that Albert Houghton standing left is at the gate of his home and workshop in North Street by the protective covering he carries round his middle which he needed while working over his boot-tree. His father George was a cobbler and farmer and his uncle Fuller was a cobbler too . Albert was also a renowned entomologist and naturalist, entirely self-taught, who had a wealth of Latin names at his disposal for the moths, butterflies, birds and plants in Wicken Fen. He served the university men, directing their activities and catching them specimens. We see him here in the 1880s with Uriah Fuller, who was born in 1832 and known as 'Tight' Fuller for obvious reasons. He was the father of John Fuller previously identified. Albert died in 1896 aged 56. He had also been the village postman and was succeeded in this by his son Morley (his mother's maiden name). After Albert's death Morley continued his cobbler's trade.

(E.S.Aspland)

SILENT NIGHTS IN THE FEN

Here is Albert Houghton in his other guise, dressed for the part with an assistant, set up for darkness - rather early tor the photographer's sake and no doubt getting a fee for it -with his lamp and sheet to attract the great variety of moths attracted to it. He built up a huge collection of moths and butterflies but they have vanished without trace, to the great concern of his dependants. He married Jemima Morley and they had seven children. The night mothcatchers were abundant in my childhood, fitting up their ghostly sheets in the open spaces, becoming as reluctant as keen fisherman to go home while there was a chance of a big catch. Albert Houghton bred a swallowtail butterfly which is still registered in his name. Looking at him here in June 1892 it is hard to believe he would die within four years.

(Birmingham Library Services; P.J. Deakin)

THE OTHER COBBLER

Peachey Johnson - always known as Petchey - had his shoemaker's shop built beside what is now 14 North Street. Later it came to be used as a sweetshop by Ellis and Mary Leonard. It has since been demolished. As well as being another cobbler living amicably yards away from the Houghtons, Petchey shoed donkeys and has just done the job on the one shown here. He was also a tobacconist and a Sunday school teacher working here from the 1890s but gone by the 1920s. There were plenty of heavy boots for these cobblers to work on, used by young and old for work, school and what leisure they could contrive and Petchey made a fair living here, warring only with builder Josiah Owers down the street. They were catalysts to each other a long time, coming to blows and settling some quarrels in court, but Petchey looks peacable enough here circa 1900.

(E.S. Aspland)

THE WESLEYANS

After inheriting the estate of her sister, Sarah Rayner of Wicken Hall, in I83I, Mary Hatch of Stuntney carried out her sister's wish to provide the tillage with schools before endowing us with almshouses in North Street. They were to be for widows or single ladies who were communicants of the Church of England and they remain in use today with modernised interiors. These are a big proportion of the Wicken Wesleyan congregation sitting before them, following the ceremony of laying the foundation stones of the new chapel next door on May 25th 1911. Reading left to right, *back*: Jemima Houghton, Elsie Bishop, Laura Taylor, Maud Coxall, unidentified, Alice Butcher, Mabel Taylor, Olley Bullman, Ernie Norman, George Bullman and baby Olga Bishop. *Middle*: Bob Scrivener, May Avey, unidentified, Jimmy Clay, Walter Bishop between two half-hidden faces, unidentified, Bill Norman, a half-face, Dorcas Palmby and her mother Mrs Reeder, George Townshend of Fordham, Mr and Mrs Arthur Bullman, Albert Taylor, Robert Bullman (the second);a half face,William Bishop, two visitors, Cyril Bishop, three visitors behind, Bertha Bailey, Ida Taylor, Elizabeth Taylor, Sarah Hawes. *Front*: Nelly Canham, Claude Canham, Munns of Soham, Doris Bishop, Hugh Bishop, Susan Norman, Mr Kernode, Granny Slack, a visiting preacher, Mr and Mrs W.D. Slack, Mr Foss, unidentified, Bertha Taylor with Kate Taylor in front, Ella Bishop, Violet Taylor and a half face. Reggie Butcher sits in front.

(Gillson, Burwell)

THE CLUB FEAST

Identifications aplenty again for the Sons of Humanity Friendly Society who met annually for their club feast in the Wesleyan Sunday school. Both landowners and workers were members, making quarterly payments to insure themselves against injury and illness, absentees to this reunion without good excuse being subjected to a fine. Two of its members were appointed monthly as pallbearers. Here they are in June 1923 seated in front of the carpentry sheds used by Josiah Owers and Sons then Bill Simpkin. *Left to right, back*: Jimmy Clay, David 'Sixfoot' Bailey, Walter Canham, Tom Rumberlow, Percy Bishop, Arthur 'Bant' Hawes, Percy 'Tiny' Bailey, Arthur Scrivener, Bob Canham, Cecil 'Roth' Delph, Albert King, John Fuller, David Canham, Arthur Bishop, Fred 'Stubby' Bailey, Bill Solly Bailey. *Third row*: George Bishop, George Butcher, Billy 'Boot' Bishop, Walter Bishop, Nathan Norman, Morley Houghton, Morley Hawes, George 'Jammy' Bullman, George Coxall, David 'Boxer' Fuller' John 'Cocky' Bailey, William 'Daddy' Bishop, Giles Bullman, Uriah Marshall, George Nixon,John 'Shop' Bailey. *Second row*: Bill Scrivener, Harry Marshall, 'Jimmy' 'Newly' Hawes, John Norman, George Day, Charlie Cranwell, Bill Norman, Albert Taylor, Jacob Taylor, Olley Bullman, George Broome, John 'Bunyan' Bailey, Jack Granfield, Jethro Granfield. *Front*: Bill 'Twinet' Simpkin, Jim 'Smoker' Bailey, Clarence Bailey, Wilfred 'Foot'Bailey, Clifford 'Tipper' Nixon, Frank Nixon, Hubert Taylor, Joshua 'Jot' Bailey, George 'Booty' Bailey, Bert Canham, George Cranwell.

(Author's collection)

JACOB'S HOME

The Sons of Humanity were gazing across the road to this cottage, Jacob Taylor's home where his wife Alice is standing at the gate. They were married on October 27th 1860, Alice being a Simpkin, sister of Susan Canham whose cottage was burned down at the time of Arthur Bullman's fire. Alice's grandson, George Bullman, later occupied this cottage and had it replaced with the bungalow that stands on the site today. Jacob Taylor, who appears on the Club Feast photograph, died later that year aged 84. He had worked for Robert Aspland in his shop at The Chestnuts and was a lay preacher who walked miles to outlying chapels on Sundays, even as far as Newmarket. Along the route home ,in season, he plucked berries from the hedges to sustain him.

(E.S. Aspland)

THE LODE

Emma Aspland spent many hours alone or with her chosen visitors clicking her camera near the mouth of Wicken Lode, or the New River as it was often described on the maps. She sensed the timeless peace of it where nevertheless, much work was done unloading the turf and sedge boats. And Solomon Bailey was never far away, another amateur student of moths and butterflies, busy at night with his sheet and lamp and net, standing here before the main tree. Emma made no attempt to catch people working since all had to be still for the lens and thus the peace of her views is enhanced. The time is the turn of the century and Emma would not have enjoyed the over-civilised order of today.

(E.S. Aspland)

THE TURF SHEDS

Opposite the previous view stood the turf sheds owned by, from the left, Josiah Owers, Bill Norman and Mark Bailey. Again peace reigns, but after the work is done and there is no-one to be ordered still. These turves came from Lapwing reaching Burwell Lode, haled down the towpath by donkeys. The turves had been dried some six weeks after digging and were collected at these sheds by turf vendors from Soham who made a far better living than the diggers, not to mention the land workers. The digging was hard yet not heavy work in the trenches in hot summer and the diggers were on piecework wages. Their season lasted, however, only from the first week in March to the last in August. The second world war finished the industry and the last of the fen turt diggers was Bert Bailey of Wicken who died at 95 in 1982.

(E.S. Aspland)

Wicken Fen.

THE LODE COTTAGES

The lode cottages formed a hamlet in themselves at the time of this photograph pointing towards the fen, and long afterwards past my childhood. Eleven families lived there at this time while the turf industry still continued but few of the cottages remain. As the National Trust purchased them they pulled them down, stopping only at a lesser example which has been restored . What a feature they might have been today as examples of the use of the local materials of sedge and reed and hard turves for insulation, some cottages going back more than two hundred years' This scene, however, is largely intact with John Butcher's cottage on the right and the restored cottage on the left. John was a turf digger. He married twice, his second wife Annie fostering three Barnardo children, two brothers and a sister, in this cottage. She undertook sewing classes for senior schoolgirls.

(Author's collection)

Lode, Wicken Fen.

LOOKING BACK UP THE LANE

The far cottage on the left was the last to go in Lode Lane, demolished and replaced with two dwellings by a private developer. The restored cottage is on the right, now back under thatch from the fen, furnished as of yore with a true cottage garden and open to visitors. George and John Butcher were brothers. George bought this cottage and let it to turf digger Lister Arthur Bailey, son of Mark, and his wife Bertha. It was then occupied by Arthur and Maud Porter, then Oswald and Edith Bailey, during whose occupancy a gale destroyed the thatch This was replaced by corrugated iron by John Sargeant, who was responsible for all such replacements in Wicken, known as 'Welsh thatch' if they were over thatch. George Butcher was farming at Field Farm on the Upware road and after his wife Ellen died in 1921 his son Robert, formerly a turf digger, and his wife Alice and son Reggie joined him there. Robert, however, died within the year aged 45 and George, Alice and Reggie moved into this lode cottage where George died in 1936 and Alice in 1972. In 1974 Reggie sold the property to the National Trust and moved into the far cottage in this picture, which he also owned. Prior to the recent development the last dwelling to be built in Lode Lane was the fen keeper's house in 1922.

(Author's collection)

COTTAGERS AND VISITORS

Here in the 1890s are four denizens of Lode Lane with four visitors, the ladies from home and away all spruced up for the camera. On the left stands Billy 'Puddn' Bailey, turf man and general labourer and George Butcher stands with stiff obedience. Behind those laundered aprons are Ann Borgus and Amelia Bailey, nee Borgus. The fen was discovered by naturalists long before it became nationally known through the National Trust and the locals took full advantage of the visits, guiding, refreshing, boarding wherever possible, accepting tips to add to their meagre incomes. Visitors came by pony, boat or on foot before the motor age and there was always food and accommodation for them in the village.

(E.S. Aspland)

THE FEN FIRE

This nothingness is Wicken Sedge Fen after the devastating fire of August I5th 1929. The whole fen was scorched peat, the wildlife gone, hopes for early regeneration very low. The first I knew of it were the bells of approaching fire engines, flame-faced charioteers at the helm, and I ran out in awe. My grandfather was due to pick me up with pony and buggy to take me to his Red Barn Farm and my pleas to be allowed to follow those fire engines were dismissed. Yet when grandfather took me away I found myself with a fair platform view of the fire creeping over the flat peat while ogreish clouds of smoke swelled above, reflecting the flames underneath. The pony shot a wild eye now and then, threatening to pull us off the road, but grandad's mind was on the safety of his harvest corn like all the farmers round about. The fire stopped at the water barriers, however, but the engines could do no more than stand by the thatch of the lode cottages. A carelessly cast match, possibly by excisemen visiting the Maid's Head and the fen, was presumed to have started the fire. The village smelt of ash for weeks.

(Cambridgeshire Collection; Reid)

ONE YEAR AFTER

This photograph, taken just one year after the fen fire, shows that the fears about its quick regeneration were groundless. Bill Barnes the fen keeper stands in the lush reeds as if the fire had never happened and although the tree felt the damage the wildlife was thriving there as before. The fen had caught fire in the I890s and when during the last war the reclamation of Adventurers' Fen for growing crops was undertaken and it was thought fit to set fire to the reeds there, a great deal of damage was done to wildlife. Subsequent apologies did nothing to condone the act, although Wicken Sedge Fen escaped damage. Once the sedge cutting had been stopped on the fen the scrub came through and flourished, since when spaces have been cleared and have been kept clear by further sedge cutting. All of the fen had been dug intensely for peat.

(Cambridgeshire Collection; Reid)

THE GAULT BOATS

River and lode banks were being constantly re-sealed or puddled with clay, or gault, from the stream itself or any other ready source such as the pits east of St. Edmund's Fen near where these boats are moored circa 1912. Aboard stands George Bullman and by the horse Giley Bailey. Monks' Lode seen here begins at Landwade Hall near Exning, crossing the Fordham-Burwell road and widening its way to Wicken Lode round St. Edmund's Fen. Just beyond the bend here can be seen the plank where a railed footbridge stands today. The pits, long since surrounded by trees, became only fishing pits in my childhood but they had been dug so deep at one end that we were ordered to stay away from them. They have been much abused since by dumping. The George Bullman here is the one who succeeded to Jacob Taylor's cottage and Giley Bailey is remembered as a fine cornet player with Wicken Band who was always entrusted with the Last Post for the Armistice Day services. He eventually moved to Histon.

(Gillson, Burwell)

SCHOOL 1891

It hardly paid a boy to be too sharp a learner at this time, since he could find himself working on the land by the age of ten. Once released at that age his parents would be reminded to send him back to school on wet days, but drought set in permanently as far as the boy was concerned. My father was sly enough to ease his way along to the maximum eleven but like almost every boy then he had to work on Saturdays. This is the senior class studying in the school bequeathed by Sarah Rayner in 1831, which lasted until 1908. Monitor Martha 'Tottie' Bishop stands left then, *left to right, back*: Ernie Norman, John Hawes, Billy Norman, Joe Harding, Mary Ellwood, Arthur Bullman, Florence Bullman, Julia Bullman. *Second row*: Ezra Bailey, Elizabeth Marshall, George Nixon, Alice Taylor, George Norman, Robert Ellwood, Eliza Delph. *First row:* Louisa. Bishop, Minnie Marshall, Nell Bishop, Nellie Taylor, Sidney Canham, Robert Taylor, Fred Bullman, Ernie Bullman. *Front*: Robert Nixon and Oliver Ellwood. The Ellwoods were the children of the then Wicken policeman, who eventually became an inspector. The teacher at the right is the severe Mary Shenessey against whom some boys staged a rebellion, cornering her, pulling her hair down and scaring her enough to force her to have a few days off, of which nothing appears in the school log. To the relief and astonishment of all she left to be married.

(Author's collection)

THE NIGHT SCHOOL 1910-11

There was a condition at this time that boys leaving school at the age of twelve should thereafter attend night school for two sessions a week, on Tuesdays and Thursdays, either until the master released them or subsequently when they chose to leave. This was the policy of Percy John Walling when he arrived as headmaster in 1906 and many older youths were uplifted at the opportunity to extend their basic knowledge or learn a new craft, my father among them. Within two years Mr Walling had secured a new school and the classes grew. The practical classes included basket making and land measurement, for which the teacher himself had attended classes. *Back*, left to right: Jack Bailey, Sidney Barton, William Scrivener (killed first world war), Mr. Walling, Fred Bullman, Percy Norman (killed first world war), Arthur Bailey (emigrated to America), Fred Owers. *Middle*: Ernie Bailey, Horace Simpkin, John Owers, George Barton, Oswald Bailey. *Front*: Arthur Scrivener, Robert Bailey, Cecil Bailey. The Owers brothers were the builder sons of Josiah who later left the village, as did Jack and Cecil Bailey, the sons of Martin.

(Author's collection)

THE GARDENING CLASS 1928

Percy Walling remained at Wicken school for forty years before retiring to Soham. He was largely self-taught as a teacher, with the help of a correspondence college and thus, to supplement his income, he continued to study carpentry and gardening during the long vacations to gain higher certificates. He passed on his knowledge to the senior boys, using the old school for woodwork and taking full advantage of the sew school's large garden. The boys loved these lessons, of course, mixing their inherited good sense with the master's science in the open air to which most of them would be drawn after leaving school at fourteen. Here, left to right are, *back*: Wilfred Harding, Hubert Taylor, Denis Porter, Joe Pope, Bob Houghton. *Front*: Joe Redit, Sid Houghton, Bob Gilbert, Eric Breed, Jack Hall, Clifford Nixon and Matthew Cranwell. The one who went on to higher education here was Joe Pope, now Sir Joseph Pope, who became an academic and was knighted for his services to industry.

(Mrs Eric Breed collection)

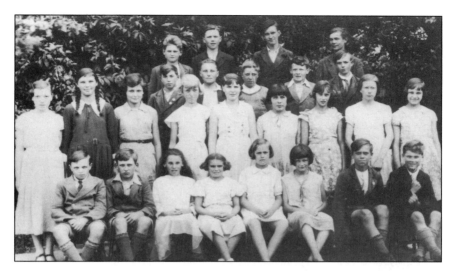

THE SENIOR CLASS 1935

Photographic souvenir groups have given us something to dwell upon when in nostalgic mood, remembering the days when we all knew each other and came from no other place. The fashion of producing them every year died out by the 1960s and thus a valuable record was lost. We were photographed individually too but these groups have survived the best. This one was my time at Wicken school, into my last year there. *Back, left to right*: Wilf Barnes, Fred Bailey (killed second world war) Jackie Grummitt, Charlie Wright. *Third row*: Les Pamment, Arthur Money, Tom Bailey, Tony Day, George Bullman. *Second row*: Margery Orchin, Jessie Clay, Eileen Blackmore, Eileen Nixon, Doll Bailey, Sylvia Redit, Joyce Earle, Edith Delph, Crystal Harding. *Front*: Stuart Canham, Peter Crow, Rhoda Hawes, Beatrice Bird, Phyllis Cross, Florrie Wright, Claude Rumberlow (killed second world war) and Roland Avey.

(Author's collection)

MRS WALLING'S CLASS 1938

Mrs Walling, nee Manning of Soham, taught with her husband from the outset, taking the middle form. The photographers rarely came into the school and this is one of only two instances of them doing so. Standing back, left to right: Phyllis Bailey, Jean Cater, Joan Delph, Phillip Bullman, Phillip Rumberlow, Bert Westley, Derrick Sargent. Two girls extreme right: Hilda Samms, Margaret McLaren. Three boys, front: John Simpkin, Bobby Douglas, Bruce Ungless. The desk behind: Charlie Harding and Godfrey Bird, then Brian Howe and Vic Williams, then Bobby Orchin and Bert Sargeant, then Cecil Dennis and Olly Bullman. Girls, front: Wendy Hawes. Desk behind: Jean Sargent, Beryl Money, then Cyril Dennis and Iris Dennis, then Pamela Robson, Miriam Westley and Cissie Delph, then unidentified, Joan Diver, Elsie Peachey and Cynthia Dennis.

(Author's collection)

PEACOCK FARM

Relaxing away from the scholastic scene we can follow Emma Aspland's picturesque walk down Chapel Lane into what was Low Drove, but now Lower Road, at the turn of the century, taking in so much that has gone. First of the missing is Peacock Farm, occupied at the turn of the century by William and Sophia Preston, who succeeded John Cropley there. William thanked divine providence when in 1865 the cattle plague ravaged through Wicken and his cows were spared. William died in 1895 and Sophia, here clinging possessively to daughter Sophie while daughter Molly (Mary) clutches the cat, died in 1914 aged 92. William Bishop moved from Upware to take over this farm and Elliot Taylor succeeded him, followed by his son Bob. Colin Unwin of the Histon seed firm bought the property and built a new Peacock House near the main road, leaving this old farmhouse to decay.

(E.S. Aspland)

JOHN HAWES' HOME

A little farther along we still call it John Hawes's Lane coming down from the main road to Lower Road. On the corner at the bottom stood his home, this fine farmhouse that looks set to stand for centuries more. Alas, it came down and my grandfather bought the land with its mixed orchard and we called it the old farm and carried home fruit by the bucketful, including plums of many colours. Mrs John Hawes and her daughter Sarah Ann dutifully pose for the scene at the end of last century. The position of the house remained visible for a long time and the perennial flowers came back. A shed remained in which I recall sheltering and shivering during a thunderstorm. The name Hawes first occurs in the parish register in 1693 and it remains here today.

(E.S. Aspland)

JOHN SEEKINGS' HOME

Next along in Low Drove was this charming house gazing out to Soham Mere. It became the home of John and Mary Seekings soon after this picture was taken but after Mary died at 29 John moved to Fordham Moor with their son Laurence. It was occupied from 1915 by Elijah Harding who had married my father's elder sister, Minnie. Later on, always on the day after Boxing Day to fit in with other family gatherings, we met here for a lavish tea and modest celebrations afterwards round the open fire. I loved the reception of this cosy house and got there early while it was still silent, but we left it for the last time in 1930 and entered their new in 1931, no doubt sharing their pride in its perfect symmetry, its high ceilings, untenanted roof and the lingering, progressive smell of new wood, plaster and paint. But what would I give to see this old house still there' It was last thatched by Brocky Aspland of Soham with sedge that was cut ripe in August to last for decades.

(E.S. Aspland)

GRAY'S FARM

Reaching the end of Low Drove as it was, past Thorne Hall which still stands if greatly altered, we reach the Padney Road, proceed past the two adjacent brick and slate houses erected for the Slack family early last century - one of them rebuilt - and arrive at Docking's Lane, which remains a rough drove. John Docking, who farmed from Gray's Farm off the drove, came from Waterbeach to marry Elizabeth Clay of Wicken in 18IO. His family name thereafter showed many alterations such as Dockens, Docken and Dorking in the parish register. This well maintained farmhouse was taken later by Harry Bailey and his son John after him and it looks in pristine condition here around I900 with Harry's daughter Polly in the proudly managed garden. After John Bailey's time the house was simply left to decay and subside and there are remains of it there now. We had a far more beautiful village once and it is as if Emma Aspland foresaw the changes for the worse.

(E.S. Aspland)

SPINNEY ABBEY c.1900

The former priory built in the reign of Henry III, rebuilt in 1775 as a dwelling, has housed four generations of the Fuller family since 1892. The first of them was Thomas Fuller who having married Sarah, one of seven daughters of King Charles who moved into High Fen Farm, farmed first at the ancestral home of the Fullers at Padney, then in Coveney. After Sarah's death in 1890 Thomas married Elizabeth Anne Ayres in 1892 then moved to Spinney in October of that year. She is standing before the abbey house here, left, with Emma Eliza, the second daughter of Thomas's first marriage, who was to marry Woollard Barton of Wicken. Spinney Abbey today also takes in boarders who will find relics of the old priory and a lot to occupy them in the private museum put together by the present Fullers, not to mention the stories of supernatural happenings.

(E.S. Aspland)

ISAAC BARROW D.D. (1614-1680)

He was the first of Wicken's three great divines, the son of Isaac Barrow and Catherine of Spinney Abbey. After more than forty years in Wicken as Justice of the Peace and squire. Isaac died in 1642 and Catherine in 1647. Isaac junior entered St. Peter's College (Peterhouse), Cambridge and took holy orders. He was ejected from his fellowship of the college for his loyalty to the Royalist cause in 1643 and he went to Oxford in 1645 to become chaplain of New College, but the fall of Oxford during the Civil War sent him into retirement. At the Restoration his fellowship of St. Pëter's was restored and he was a candidate for the mastership but lost out to Joseph Beaumont. He was made a fellow of Eton College and Rector of Little Downham, but in 1663 he was made Bishop of Sodor and Man and later its governor. Isaac put immense effort into the welfare of the island and then was translated to St. Asalph, the tiny cathedral in Flintshire built on the site of two earlier cathedrals in 1480. There he founded almshouses in 1678 but died on midsummer's day two gears later and was buried in the churchyard. His nephew, also Isaac, whose father Thomas had been linen draper to Charles I, outstripped him in fame as a divine and became Master of Trinity College, Cambridge.

(From the original painting in Peterhouse College, Cambridge.)

HENRY CROMWELL (1628-1674)

It is ironic that one so identified with the Commonwealth cause should follow the Royalist presence in Spinney Abbey, but in the person of Henry Cromwell, the former Protector's fourth and most worthy son, it was no matter. He had served his father well in Ireland during the Civil War, becoming Lord Lieutenant of Ireland, and now wanted that far behind him after the Restoration to live the life of a country gentleman. Henry had spent his youth in Ely, living in the Cromwell house at St Mary's Green, which is now open to the public to display the Cromwellian period in domestic detail. Henry had married Elizabeth Russell of Chippenham Hall and they had seven children, but with his life settled at Spinney Henry died aged 46. His family experienced hardship thereafter. His son Oliver succeeded and then Oliver's widow for two years, followed by Henry junior who was forced to mortgage the estate. Henry and Elizabeth and other descendants are buried in Wicken church and a wooden screen to commemorate them was placed in the church by succeeding members of the family. The original painting from which this print was taken was by Christian Desart and it was sold from a London saleroom in the I970s to an Italian dealer in 'Old Britannia.'

(Courtauld Institute of Art.)

SHEEP AT SPINNEY

Robert Fuller was the first farmer in Wicken to use a car to reach his workers. A Sunbeam acquired in 1916 it was familiar for being unusual in Wicken for a long time. Robert used it too in the service of voters, lifting them to the polling station in the certainty they would vote his way. Here he is in 1926 sitting in the car on a visit to his shepherds with two visitors, Frank Jeffrey with his mother-in-law May Hawes, wife of Todd formerly of Wicken. Todd's brother Albert of Ash Tree Farm and High Fen Farm was the other farmer who found sheep economical in the village, having the necessary space. His shepherd was Billy Day. At Spinney it was Tom Delph, standing left with Jim Jopson his assistant, and Tom's son Sid with the visitors behind ,watching the sheep begin a new feasting ground. Sheep performed the useful service of fertilizing the land and, indeed, for that purpose and to crop the first growth of spring in order to strengthen the roots for better growth, they were sometimes driven over crops of winter wheat.

(Eunice Fuller)

THE END OF THE WORKING DAY

Back down to the Padney road, which was firmer beyond Low Drove, and on past Ash Tree Farm we arrive at Sheepwalk where, indeed, sheep, cattle and horses with men in tow passed for generations. It leads to High Fen, Red Barn Farm and the Upware corner, but farther down the Padney road on the right were rich pastures going down to Soham Mere, known as The Dolvers. Here on Slate Dolver we witness the scene that generally ended every farmer's working day. The farmer has arrived with pony and cart to do the evening milking and this one with four cows will have milk and butter to sell, as did my grandfather with three cows although they were firstly for domestic use. The grass was high here and the hedges were high and thick to feed the cattle their chosen medicine and the trees spread to give shade. There would be a churn in the cart and a water supply from the ditches and the farmer would have to refill the tank using a scoop before going home to turn the separator.

(Author's collection)

ANDREW FULLER (1754-1815)

We reach Padney, now a small group of dwellings, once the sole preserve of the Fuller family who settled there in the late I7th century. John the first arrival was followed by his son Robert, born I696, who built the Padney Farmhouse that still stands, albeit with the original thatch replaced by tiles. Robert had four sons and a daughter and one of the sons was Andrew who became a famous Baptist minister, firstly at the Baptist chapel in Soham and then at Gold Street, Kettering, where the chapel still carries his esteemed name. Andrew also became the first secretary of the Baptist Missionary Society and was recognised as one of the outstanding national figures of that faith who had some influence on the Reverend Robert Aspland before they went their separate ways. Padney Farm continues to be farmed by the Fullers, the present generation being Brian who has no sons. The route beyond provided a difficult way out of Wicken before the rivers Cam and Old West were bridged in 1928 and most travellers-went back the way they came. The other route out into sometimes difficult droves was over the ferry at Upware.

(Author's collection)

THE MILITARY ROAD

Until the first world war the route beyond the Upware corner and Red Barn Farm was no more than a drove ending at the river, to go beyond which the traveller would have to cross by stepping stones on to a boat. Then came the national need to transport army vehicles and troops that way and the road was reinforced with hardcore taken from pits near the Fodder Fen drove and this pontoon bridge was placed across the Cam. A few local men made good money digging and transporting the marl. By the summer of 1917 all maintenance work on the road was abandoned and there were complaints that it should be left to deteriorate and grow over and not be taken further with permanent bridges to create a main route through the village. Tell that to those living close to the street in Wicken today! The bridges were built between 1926 and 1928 and opened almost at the same time and this is still known as the Military Road, while the pits have been and are still being used for dumping or further excavation.

(Cambridgeshire Collection)

THE OLD WEST

This scene from ninety years ago showing the old route across Stretham Mere arriving at the Old West river is totally recognisable today. The cottage remains where a new and wider bridge has replaced that of 1928. Until that time the people of Stretham and Wicken were comparative strangers to one another, although a few marital ties were made between them. There were closer ties between Wicken and Waterbeach which was accessible across the ferry at Upware and the quickest route to Cambridge by pony and cart, bicycle or on foot, discounting a walk or ride to Burwell across the fen to take the train to Barnwell Junction which was the way my grandfather travelled to Cambridge cattle market.

(Cambridgeshire Collection)

THE FIVE MILES

On then to Upware, the road to which has been well maintained since the ferry was added to the amenities of the inn built by the river in 1811. There have never been but droves on the other side. The Lord Nelson became the No Hurry - Five Miles from Anywhere from the 1860s, so dubbed by Richard Ramsey Fielder, a rumbustious graduate and poet of Cambridge who loved to join the steady drinkers here. My grandparents kept the inn between 1901 and 1916 and their daughter for two years after that and they charged the following fees for the ferry they hired from the brewers for seven pounds a year: For a person on foot, one penny; with a bicycle, twopence; with pony and trap, fourpence; with horse and cart, sixpence and with cattle, twopence a head. Too many heads at a time sank the ferry sometimes' Ben Read, who was not my natural grandfather, stands here, right, with William Farren the Cambridge photographer whose brother Robert was a fen painter and etcher of distinction who spent much time' in Wicken. Originally under thatch, the hugely popular Five Miles caught fire in 1956 and was demolished in 1957. The site stood empty but for the floor tiles still showing for a long time before the new inn was placed on the site, carrying the old name.

(Author's collection)

HIS MAJESTY OF UPWARE, 1860s

Out of the mists of time appears the inscrutable face of Richard Ramsey Fielder, a youthful Falstaffian figure in his wild moments at Upware, a show-off there who had himself painted in oils while clearly insisting on a flamboyant image far from the visible truth of this photograph. He styled himself 'His Majesty of Upware' in reaction to the claims of a Cambridge University group of a decade earlier who described themselves as the Upware Republic and tried to appear as disreputable as possible. Samuel Butler was one of them. Fielder, however, was merely diverting himself at Upware, for he was a man of learning and deep sincerity, a student of fen drainage and a prolific poet modelling his style on that of Shakespeare. He eventually 'foreswore sack' to live a sober life in Folkstone.

(Cambridgeshire collection)

THE SUNDAY SCHOOL OUTING

Almost enough aboard here to sink the Upware ferry! It is summer 1906 and the annual outing to exotic Upware for the Sunday school children, including tea in a barn. From 1923 members of the church choir preferred a charabanc trip to the seaside but the Cam remained the sea for these bible students. The vicar and his aides found no difficulty in keeping order. Left to right they are: Peachey Johnson, the Reverend Ernest Dibben, Maria Knowles, Miss Gussy Dibben and Helena Hawes whose daughters Annie and Amy are in white in front of her. To the right are Tom Hall with Jim Hawes behind him, George Barton, Arthur Hall and John Bullman. Harriet Hawes stands extreme right. At the back, standing high are George Hawes, Bob Hawes and Fred Hawes. Next to them at the back is Sybil Kettle while Lizzie Bailey stands next to Anna Cockrill at the fight. The Upware schoolteacher, Mrs Pratt, lived in the cottage behind.

(Author's collection)

THE UPWARE CRICKET TEAM, 1910

If the ground conditions were not quite suitable for the subtle leg glance across the surface it was great for the agricultural swipe - so long as it was not into the all-too-adjacent river' Not surprisingly many of the male inhabitants of Upware, which was a closely-knit community at this time, made the Five Miles the centre of their lives - and not just for drinking. There was good food there from home-grown produce and sometimes good homemade entertainment and enough of them came together to form a cricket team to face the likes of Reach one long drove away. Some were younger than they look here, but none was too old to run or dive in quickly to avoid being run out. *Left to right at the back:* Walter Cornwell, Bert Housden and Mr Pratt the schoolteacher's husband who lived apart from her. *Middle:* Ben Read, Mr Mole, Arthur Stevens, Walter Housden and Frank Gurry. *Front:* Ernie Clark, skipper of *The Nancy* a pleasure boat then, Jack Howe and Bill King with mascot Nigel Read in front. Field placings and batting order are unknown - and probably were to them.

(John Layton)

THE SKATING CHAMPION

The aforementioned Walter Houeden (1873-1953) farmed at Duckett Farm, Upware, just into Swaffham Fen. The Cam floodbank rose across the rough road outside his front door and over that bank the floods froze in winter and Walter, from an early age, took to the ice. So did many another Upware resident, warming their blood most when the weather was cold, but none could keep up with Walter on skates. He became the Amateur Skating Champion of Great Britain in 1891 and might have retained it if he had not decided to turn professional to make himself some money while young. As such he was also very successful, although he never won the professional championship. In the consecutive races for it between 1895 and 1908 he finished third, third, second, third and second again. He also won the prestigious Hayes Fisher Cup over three miles at Littleport in 1895 over thirteen competitors, a race, however, that was not staged again until 1929 when, at 56, Walter entered, exceeded his old winning time by two seconds yet was unplaced. He was still on the ice in his seventies, able to skate backwards faster than most going forwards in this community.

(Cyril West collection)

71

THE SWAFFHAM ENGINE

This magnificent pumping engine, so essential to the drainage of the area, would have been an enormous attraction today had it been allowed to stand. It was built at the head of the Swaffham Drain at Upware in 1851, replacing a station built in 1821. Nearby, on the other side of Burwell Lode on Commissionaires' Drain was the Burwell engine also built in 1821, the shell of which still stands. The Stevens family saw out the days of the Swaffham engine. William came in from Little Downham's Hundredfoot engine to become both superintendent of drainage and engineer and his son Arthur succeeded him as engineer. Diesel replaced steam in 1927 and Arthur found this irksome and retired. His brother Charles had assisted him as had Charlie Bullman and Arthur's son Jim took over for a short time. But this structure, seen here around 1910, was demolished in 1939. The diesel shed remains with the new shed and its modern apparatus. The Swaffham engine survived a bad fire in the 1890s, thanks to the courage of William Stevens, for it was essential to keep this great beam engine with its scoopwheels going night and day. My father lifted me up to that haunting window when I was a child, but I never went inside.

(Author's collection)

PRIOR FEN POST OFFICE

Three miles from the centre of Wicken, Upware within the parish received its food supplies from both sides of the river, from Wicken, Soham and Waterbeach. Between the wars Walter Cracknell delivered groceries from over the ferry, sometimes in snowbound winter carrying them with help on a stretcher along the river bank. Within the hamlet Mrs Dick Creek, matriarch of the Creek family settled around Upware who came in from Sheffield, kept a shop, post office and cafe within The Anchor public house between the pumping stations. Accessible also to the tiny population was this Prior Fen shop and post office near the Swaffham Fen chapel. Ernie Clark of *The Nancy* kept it, followed by Henry Stamford, farmer, and his family for a long time and under its glorious cover of vines and cushioned in trees and bushes, including a white elderberry, it was an enchanting port of call. The Stamfords later bought the adjacent chapel to keep it open, at least once a year for harvest festivals. By that chapel was a shed in which our postman of the 1930s, Tommy Hood, mended shoes collected on his delivery round, thus profitably using the time-gap needed before his collections.

(Author's collection)

THE EMIGRANTS

For some, inevitably, there had to be more than hard work on the land for life in our small isolated fen village. More profitable jobs farther away appealed. Some left to work in the mines or on the railways and from the middle of last century a tradition of emigration had grown within the village. Rosy messages home tempted others to go to Australia, Canada and America and only in one instance, to my knowledge, did it not work out. Bill and Jemima Simpkin set forth to America but were back within weeks, luckily having the funds to return, and there was no more settled man in Wicken thereafter than Bill our carpenter, although having sold my father his family clock before leaving he almost wept, vainly, to have it back again. The message for Bill and Lizzie Norden to go to America came from her sister Mina who had settled nicely there earlier. Thus they embarked on the *Mauretania* in 1923 and we see them aboard here with daughter Jessie, seemingly full of the sadness of leaving while hardly daring to think ahead. But they too settled comfortably, keeping in touch with Lizzie's parents, Bill and Emma Bailey of Butts Lane, and the village was not forgotten by their descendants.

(Dorothy Johnson collection)